PRIZEWINNING ANIMALS

PRIZEWINNING HORSES

Nancy Greenwood

PowerKiDS press

NEW YORK

Published in 2023 by The Rosen Publishing Group, Inc.
29 East 21st Street, New York, NY 10010

First Edition

Portions of this work were originally authored by Jennifer Wendt and published as *Blue Ribbon Animals: Showing Horses at the Fair.* All new material in this edition was authored by Nancy Greenwood.

Editor: Kate Mikoley
Book Design: Andrea Davison-Bartolotta

Photo Credits: Cover Zuzule/Shutterstock.com; series art (animal outlines) Picture Window/Shutterstock.com; series art (gold ticket) Mar1kOFF/Shutterstock.com; series art (red ribbon) FMStox/Shutterstock.com; series art (pennant banner, gold ribbon) Tiax/Shutterstock.com; pp. 5, 15 AnnaElizabeth photography/Shutterstock.com; p. 6 meunierd/Shutterstock.com; p. 7 Osetrik/Shutterstock.com; p. 9 Makarova Viktoria/Shutterstock.com; p. 11 James Clark/Shutterstock.com; p. 12 Sari ONeal/Shutterstock.com; p. 13 Konstantin Tronin/Shutterstock.com; p. 14 D Barton/Shutterstock.com; p. 17 Fotokostic/Shutterstock.com; p. 19 My Good Images/Shutterstock.com; p. 21 acceptphoto/Shutterstock.com.

Library of Congress Cataloging-in-Publication Data

Names: Greenwood, Nancy, author.
Title: Prizewinning horses / Nancy Greenwood.
Description: New York : PowerKids Press, [2023] | Series: Prizewinning animals | Includes index.
Identifiers: LCCN 2021040087 | ISBN 9781538386309 (set) | ISBN 9781538386316 (library binding) | ISBN 9781538386293 (paperback) | ISBN 9781538386323 (ebook)
Subjects: LCSH: Horses–Showing–Juvenile literature.
Classification: LCC SF294.7 .G74 2023 | DDC 636.1/0811–dc23
LC record available at https://lccn.loc.gov/2021040087

Manufactured in the United States of America

Some of the images in this book illustrate individuals who are models. The depictions do not imply actual situations or events.

CPSIA Compliance Information: Batch #CSPK23. For Further Information contact Rosen Publishing, New York, New York at 1-800-237-9932.

CONTENTS

Showing YOUR HORSE

If you want to learn more about horses, getting involved with a horse show at your local fair might be a good way to do it. From different styles of riding to training your horse, there's a lot you can learn through helping your horse become a prizewinning animal.

Showing any animal takes a lot of time and hard work. But through the work, you will learn things you never knew before. You may even make new friends along the way!

Showing your horse will teach you some of the best ways to care for it.

Ways TO RIDE

The two main riding styles in a horse show are English and Western. In Western riding, the **saddle** is bigger and more comfortable. It also has a horn in front for you to hold onto.

In English riding, the saddle is smaller and lighter. Riders commonly wear fitted jackets and tall boots. Some people think English riding is harder to learn than Western. You'll need to decide which style you want to **compete** in before you start training.

ROAD TO WINNING

English riders often wear a coat, shirt, **jodhpurs**, boots, and a helmet. Western riders often wear a shirt, tie, belt, jeans, boots, and a helmet.

Western riders sometimes wear a cowboy hat and cowboy boots.

Time TO TRAIN

After you've picked which riding style you want to do, you can start training! You should work with your horse several times a week. If you're a beginner, make sure to have an adult nearby in case you need help.

A fair guide will tell you what the judges at your show will be looking for. This will help you train with your horse. If you know what to expect on the big day, you can stay **focused** on the show.

Horses are very smart animals. It's important to keep them busy with toys so they don't get bored.

Preparing YOUR HORSE

Like any living thing, your horse's health is important. Find out what **vaccinations** your horse needs in order to take part in the show. Bring any paperwork with you to show the fair officials.

To get to the fair, your horse will ride in a **trailer**. If your horse hasn't been in a trailer much before, it might be scary for them. Practice loading and unloading them well before the day of the show.

If you're having trouble getting your horse in the trailer, try using a treat to get them to go in.

Looking GOOD!

Some tools you'll need to **groom** your horse are brushes, a facecloth, a **hoof pick**, and a comb. You should groom your horse before and after riding. Brushing should be done in the same direction that the hair grows. This removes dirt and makes your horse look nice and neat.

Give your horse a bath right before the fair. If your horse has any white spots, be sure to use whitening shampoo. This will make the white spots look clean and bright.

ROAD TO WINNING

You'll be judged on how your horse looks, so don't forget to clean their ears, eyes, nose, and hooves.

CLEANING A HOOF

Grooming your horse is about more than making them look good. It also helps form a bond between you two.

Keep Things CLEAN

Tack is what you use to ride your horse, such as a saddle and **bridle**. Take some time before the show to clean your tack. You'll want to make sure it's all clean and in good shape before you head to the fair.

Wipe down your horse's saddle and bridle, and check for any cracks, rips, or broken **buckles** before the day of the fair. The last thing you want is to have to find new gear the day of the show!

ROAD TO WINNING

Storing your tack in a cool, dry place will help to keep it in good shape.

Remember where the buckles on the saddle and bridle are set so they'll still fit your horse the right way after you clean them.

The Day OF THE SHOW

It's the big day! Time to load your horse into the trailer. Don't forget to grab all your tack, grooming tools, horse food, and show clothes. You'll need your horse's vaccination records and fair registration papers too.

When you arrive at the fairgrounds, check in and find your **stall**. Give your horse clean bedding and fresh food and water. If possible, bring your horse to the show ring and get them used to the space.

ROAD TO WINNING

Your horse shouldn't be wearing any new or unfamiliar gear on show day. They should already be used to anything they need.

Bringing your horse to the show ring before the show can help them feel more comfortable and do their best later when being judged.

It's SHOWTIME!

It's your turn to show your horse! You should both look clean and put together. Always wear a helmet when you're riding. Look the judges in the eye and answer questions about your horse clearly.

Have fun, and don't worry if something goes wrong. If you stay calm, your horse likely will too. A big part of showing a horse is staying in control. Show the judges how well you and your horse work together.

ROAD TO WINNING

When you're done in the show ring, thank the judges and return your horse to their stall.

If you and your horse have a good bond, the judges will likely be able to tell.

Time to GO HOME

Everyone in the show is hoping to go home with a ribbon. But sadly, not everyone can win one. Whether you win or not, showing your horse at the fair is still lots of fun!

When it's time to leave, clean out your stall and pack up your grooming tools, tack, and anything else you brought. Don't forget to thank everyone who helped you. Finally, load your horse into the trailer. It's time to head home and get ready for the next show!

ROAD TO WINNING

If you can, talk to the judges after the show. Ask what you did well and what you can work on. This will help you do better next time.

There are lots of ribbon colors at a horse show. Blue is for first place.

GLOSSARY

bridle: A device that fits on a horse's head and that is used for guiding and controlling the horse.

buckle: A metal or plastic part that is attached to one end of a belt or strap and that is used to connect it to the other end.

compete: To try to win an event or contest.

focus: To direct your attention and effort at one thing in particular.

groom: To clean.

hoof pick: A tool used to clean dirt or other objects out of animal hooves.

jodhpurs: Tight pants that are worn for horseback riding.

saddle: A leather-covered seat that is put on the back of a horse.

stall: An enclosed area in a building where a farm animal, such as a horse or cow, is kept.

trailer: A large box with wheels that can be pulled behind a truck or car to transport things.

vaccination: A shot that keeps a person or animal from getting a certain sickness.

FOR MORE INFORMATION

BOOKS

Aswell, Sarah. *Intro to Show Jumping*. Minneapolis, MN: Abdo Publishing, 2018.

Harkrader, Lisa. *Horse Riding Instructor*. North Mankato, MN: Bright Idea Books, 2019.

Meister, Cari. *American Saddlebred Horses*. Mankato, MN: Amicus, 2019.

WEBSITES

4-H
4-h.org
Through hands-on projects, 4-H encourages children to learn new skills, including caring for and riding horses.

Horse
www.ducksters.com/animals/horse.php
Learn more about these amazing animals here.

Horseback Riding
www.dkfindout.com/us/sports/horseback-riding/
This website has lots of facts about horses and horseback riding.

INDEX